UPDOG↑

TRUE CRIME CLUES

CRIME SCENE INVESTIGATORS

GRACE CAMPBELL

Lerner Publications ◆ Minneapolis

Lerner Publications Company
An imprint of Lerner Publishing Group, Inc.
241 First Avenue North
Minneapolis, MN 55401 USA

For reading levels and more information, look up this title at www.lernerbooks.com.

Main body text set in ITC Franklin Gothic Std.
Typeface provided by International Typeface Corp.

Editor: Rebecca Higgins **Designer:** Kim Morales **Photo Editor:** Rebecca Higgins
Lerner team: Martha Kranes

Library of Congress Cataloging-in-Publication Data

Names: Campbell, Grace, 1993– author.
Title: Crime scene investigators / Grace Campbell.
Description: Minneapolis, MN : Lerner Publications Company, [2021] | Series: True crime clues | Includes bibliographical references and index. | Audience: Ages 8–13. | Summary: "A forensic investigator arrives to a crime scene and searches for clues. It's up to them to discover exactly what happened. This book uncovers the life of a forensic investigator and how they crack cases"— Provided by publisher.
Identifiers: LCCN 2019029623 | ISBN 9781541590564 (library binding) | ISBN 9781728414157 (pbk) | ISBN 9781728401379 (ebk pdf)
Subjects: LCSH: Crime scene searches—Juvenile literature. | Forensic sciences— Juvenile literature.
Classification: LCC HV8073.8 .C3584 2021 | DDC 363.25—dc23

LC record available at https://lccn.loc.gov/2019029623

Manufactured in the United States of America
1-47575-48105-10/29/2019

EVIDENCE

CONTENTS

Fingerprint Powder

EVIDENCE IDENTIFICATION

Date

Time

Test For ☐ DNA/SEROLOGY ☐ FIREARMS Case No
        ☐ DRUGS   ☐ IMPRESSIONS
        ☐ FINGERPRINTS ☐ QUESTIONED DOCUMENTS ☐ TOXICOLOGY
                                   ☐ TRACE EVIDENCE
Description of Evidence   ☐ OTHER
Location Collected
☐Arrest   ☐Seized   ☐Found   ☐Other
Victim/Incident
Remarks/Details
Agency
                    Signed

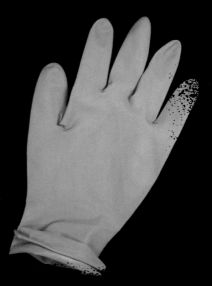

WHO ARE CRIME SCENE INVESTIGATORS?

CRIME SCENE - DO NOT CROSS   CRIME SCENE - DO NOT CROSS   CRIME SCENI

Crime scene investigators help solve
crimes. They figure out what happened.

investigators: people
who solve crimes

Some of them trained to be police officers.
Some of them studied science or pathology.

pathology: the study of diseases

UP NEXT!
THE SCENE OF THE CRIME.

CROSS   POLICE LINE DO NOT CROSS
POLICE LINE DO NOT CROSS   POL

WHAT'S AT A CRIME SCENE?

Crime scene investigators arrive to study a crime scene. They wear special gloves and suits to avoid contamination. Investigators look for evidence.

contamination: the introduction of harmful, new elements

evidence: a sign that shows something is true

They get information from detectives and people in the area.

UP NEXT!

DISCOVER A REAL CASE.

CROSS POLICE LINE DO NOT CROSS
POLICE LINE DO NOT CROSS POL

In 2001, a body was found in the woods of West Yorkshire, England. Investigators found dog hair on the corpse. They tested the hair for DNA. They found the dog's owner, who hunted in that area.

DNA: a substance that carries genetic information

UP NEXT!

EVIDENCE GOES TO THE LAB.

POLICE LINE DO NOT CROSS POLICE LINE DO NOT CROSS

POLICE LINE DO NOT CROSS POL

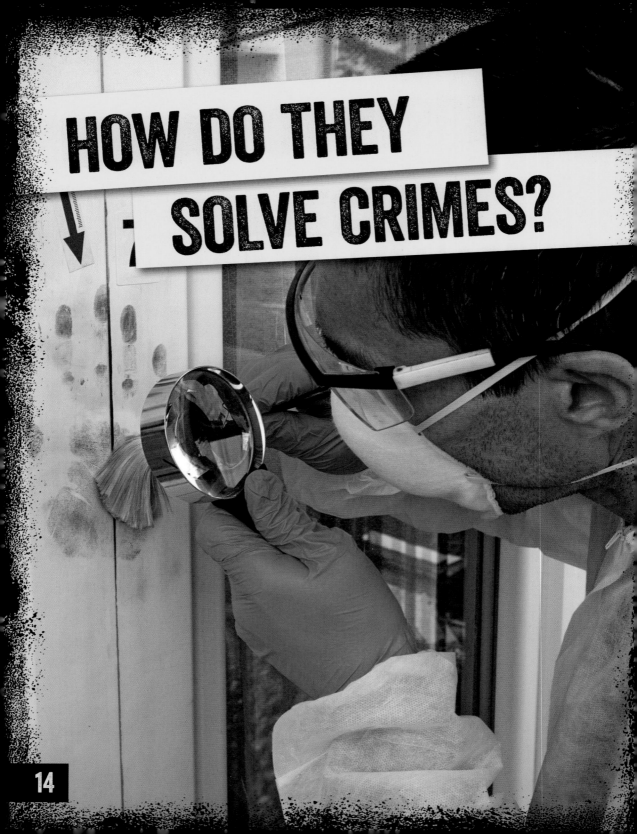

HOW DO THEY SOLVE CRIMES?

Crime scene investigators try to figure out what crime took place. They want to find the suspect.

suspect: someone who may have committed a crime

Investigators take their evidence back to a
lab for testing. They look for DNA. DNA is
found in hair, blood, or skin.

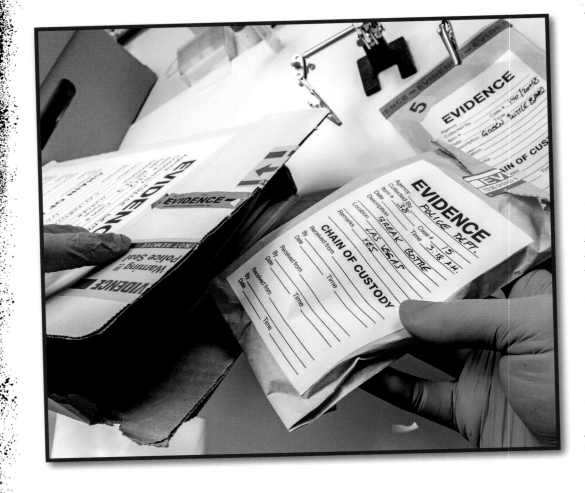

CRIME SCENE-DO NOT E

Crime scene investigators want to find a match to the DNA. Then they will have a suspect.

Crime scene investigators find who did it and solve the crime.

YOU'RE THE DETECTIVE

A bank has just been robbed. People say the suspects were wearing masks. One of the suspects had long, dark hair. Detective, what will you look for first?

A. dropped masks
B. hairs on the ground
C. money

Answer: B. hairs on the ground. DNA in the hair leads to a suspect.

GLOSSARY

contamination: the introduction of harmful, new elements

DNA: a substance that carries genetic information

evidence: a sign that shows something is true

investigators: people who solve crimes

pathology: the study of diseases

suspect: someone who may have committed a crime

CHECK IT OUT!

Carmichael, L. E. *Discover Forensic Science.* Minneapolis: Lerner Publications, 2017.
Learn more about the science behind solving crimes.

Easy Science for Kids
https://easyscienceforkids.com/forensic-science-facts/
Get a quick overview of forensic science history and facts.

Johnson, C. M. *Forensics.* Fremont, CA: Full Tilt, 2018.
Find out even more about what goes into investigating crimes.

Kids Ahead
http://kidsahead.com/subjects/3-forensics
Read articles about forensics and interviews with scientists, and try your own experiments.

Messner, Kate, and Anne Ruppert. *Solve This: Forensics.* Washington, DC: National Geographic Kids, 2020.
Try hands-on activities to test your science skills.

Mocomi
https://mocomi.com/forensic-science/
Learn more about how forensic investigators work together to solve crimes.

INDEX

PHOTO ACKNOWLEDGMENTS

Image credits: ktsimage/Getty Images, throughout (DNA); ulimi/Getty Images, throughout (frame); jamesjames2541, throughout (fingerprint); ABDESIGN/ Getty Images, pp. 2-3; D-Keine/Getty Images, pp. 4, 8; South_agency/ Getty Images, pp. 5, 20; Hill Street Studios/Getty Images, p. 6 (police); SeventyFour/Getty Images, p. 6 (pathology); stevanovicigor/Getty Images, pp. 7, 11, 13; zoka74/Getty Images, pp. 9, 14; Yuri_Arcurs/Getty Images, p. 10; WestWindGraphics/Getty Images, p. 12 (woods); digicomphoto/Getty Images, pp. 12 (hair), 16; shironosov/Getty Images, p. 15; skynesher/Getty Images, p. 17; Monty Rakusen/Getty Images, p. 18; Andrew Brookes/Getty Images, p. 19; pawel.gaul/Getty Images, p. 21 (bank); Nickondr/Getty Images, p. 21 (mask); pixhook/Getty Images, p. 21 (money); dimarik/Getty Images, p. 21 (hair).

Cover: anthonysp/Getty Images (investigator), ktsimage/Getty Images (DNA), ulimi/Getty Images (frame), stevanovicigor/Getty Images (back).